May this journal inspire you be your own
kind of wild.

-Nini

TO THE PERSON HOLDING THIS;

I made this book because whenever I would write lists or journal, I'd find myself coloring and doodling around the page, to make things more "interesting" and inspire myself.

I never saw anything that combined coloring and journaling, so I went to work creating it, because it was something that I personally wanted.

Designed to help stimulate (not squash) your creativity.

For the person who hates being put in a box, this is for you.

I hope it magnifies your sparks and relaxes your heart.

Drawn by hand, made with love, from one creative soul to another.

NINI MARIE

The World is not in your books and maps. It's out there.

THE HOBBIT

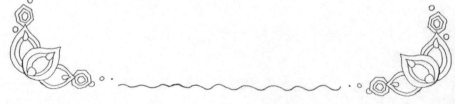

There are far better things ahead than the ones we
leave behind.

C.S.LEWIS

Adopt the pace of nature; her secret is patience.

RALPH W. EMERSON

At the center of your being you have the answer; you know who you are and you know what you want.

LAO TZU

Love is a Wild Thing

Kacey Musgraves

I don't want to earn my living, I want to live

OSCAR WILDE

Listen to Silence. It has much to say

RUMI

Wheresoever you go, go with all your heart

CONFUSCIUS

You see things and say 'why?'. But I dream things and
say 'why not?'

GEORGE BERNARD SHAW

When nothing is certain, anything is possible.

MINDY HALE

The price of anything is the amount of life you exchange for it.

HENRY DAVID THOREAU

Use your fear...it can take you to the place where you
store your courage

AMELIA EARHART

And now you are and I am and we are a mystery which
will never happen again.

E.E.CUMMINGS

There are some who can live without wild things, and
some who cannot

ALDO LEOPOLD

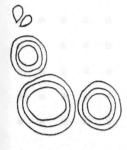

Walt Whitman

You don't have to explain your dreams, they belong to you.

PAULO COELHO

I am not afraid.
I was born to do this.

JOAN OF ARC

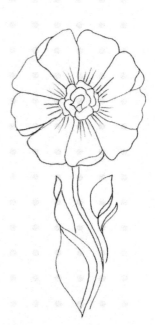

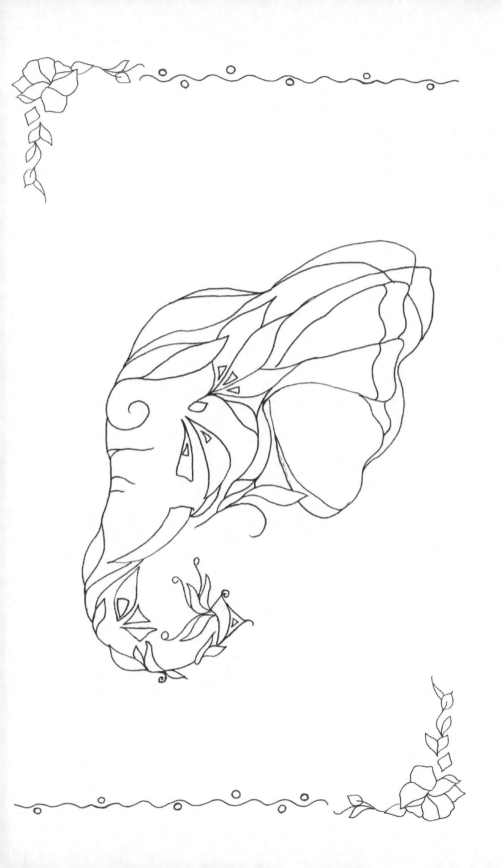

True knowledge exists in knowing that you know
nothing.

C.S.LEWIS

Once a year, go someplace you've never been before.

DALAI LAMA

Growth
Must be
Choosen again
& Again
fear
must be
overcome again
& Again

Abraham Maslow

You will see in the world what you carry in your heart.

CREIG CRIPPEN

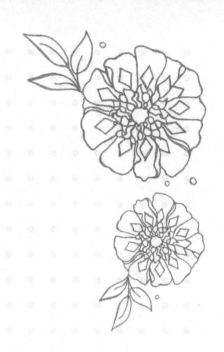

May your choices reflect your hopes, not your
fears.

NELSON MANDELA

All that we are is the result of all that we have thought.

BUDDHA

I hope you are blessed
with a heart like a wildflower.

NIKITA GILL

Do the thing you think you cannot do.

ELEANOR ROSEVELT

Never give up. When your heart becomes tired, just walk with your legs- but move on."

PAULO COELHO

Look deep into nature, and then you will understand
everything better.

ALBERT EINSTEIN

Let the Beauty you Love be what you Do.

Rumi

Everything you can imagine is real.

PABLO PICASSO

All good things are wild and free.

HENRY DAVID THOREAU

Great things are done by a series of small things
brought together.

VINCENT VAN GOGH

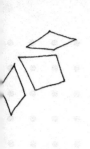

And now that
you don't
have to
be
Perfect,

You can
be
Good.

John Steinbeck

Anyone who thinks fallen leaves are dead has never
watched them dancing on a windy day.

SHIRA TAMIR

All the trees are losing their leaves, and not one of
them is worried.

DONALD MILLER

The earth has music for those who listen.

SHAKESPEARE

You were born with wings.
Why prefer to crawl through life?

RUMI

Live in the sunshine. Swim in the sea. Drink the wild air.

EMERSON

Forever is Composed
of Nows

Emily Dickenson

When you talk, you are only repeating what you already know. But if you listen, you may learn something new.

DALAI LAMA

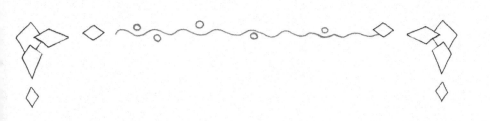

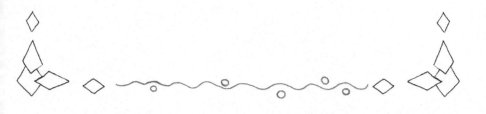

Some people feel the rain. Others just get wet.

BOB MARLEY

The world is full of magic things, patiently waiting for our senses to grow sharper.

W.B YEATS

Always go too far because that's where you'll find truth.

ALBERT CAMUS

All we have to decide is what to do with the time that is given us.

J.R.R. TOLKIEN

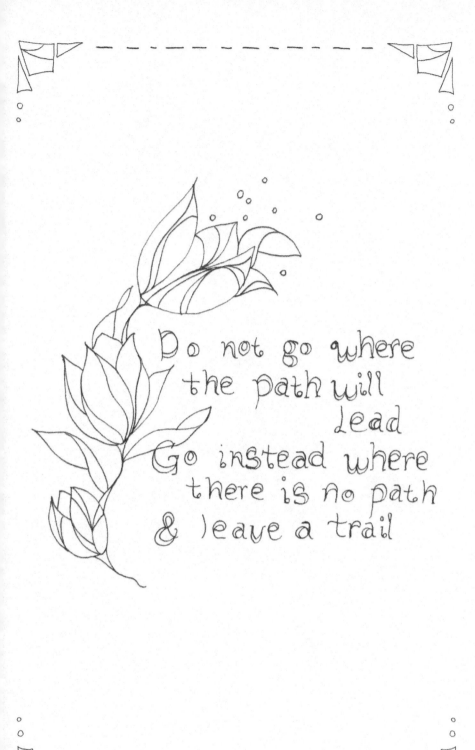

Do not go where
the path will
lead
Go instead where
there is no path
& leave a trail

Ralph Waldo Emerson

I think I'm quite ready for another adventure.

BILBO BAGGINS

Made in the USA
Las Vegas, NV
30 January 2024

85100361R00121